GENERATION

GENERATION

POEMS BY SHARON KRAUS

Alice James Books
Farmington, Maine

LIBRARY OF CONGRESS CATALOGING-IN-PUBLICATION DATA
Kraus, Sharon, 1961-
    Generation : poems / by Sharon Kraus.
        p.   cm.
    ISBN 1-882295-14-5
    I. Title
PS3561.R2884G46 1997
811'.54—dc21   97-18674
                                CIP

COVER ART: Kiki Smith, *Untitled*, 1988
            (gampi paper and methyl cellulose; life size)
            Courtesy of The Pace Gallery
COVER PHOTOGRAPH: George Rehsteiner
AUTHOR PHOTOGRAPH: Brian Murphy
BOOK DESIGN: Gillian Drake

Excerpt from *Housekeeping* by Marilynne Robinson.
Copyright © 1981 by Marilynne Robinson.
Reprinted by permission of Farrar, Straus & Giroux, Inc.

Alice James Books gratefully acknowledges support from the
University of Maine at Farmington and the
National Endowment for the Arts.

Alice James Books are published by the
ALICE JAMES POETRY COOPERATIVE, INC.
Alice James Books
98 Main Street
Farmington, Maine 04938

PRINTED IN USA

For Jacobus Schmidt

Acknowledgments

Grateful acknowledgment is made to the editors of the following publications in which these poems first appeared, sometimes in slightly different form:

Agni: "The Gesture"; *Alaska Quarterly Review*: "Geniture" (under a different title); *The Amaranth Review*: "My Mother Bathing" and "A Pardon"; *Columbia: A Journal of Literature and Art*: "What the Door Gives Onto"; *The Lowell Review*: "At the open air cafe a friend"; *The Mississippi Review*: "Rubbing My Father's Back"; *Northeast Corridor*: "Loving My Mother"; *Poetry London Newsletter*: "The Scar"; *Snake Nation Review*: "What I Could Not Save"; *Southern Poetry Review*: "Penance" and "The Girls' Home"; *The Sow's Ear Poetry Review*: "The Coroner's Assistant"; *TriQuarterly*: "The Scar" and "Transgressor"; and *Wolf Head Quarterly*: "Flight Delayed by Fog."

"The Visit" was first published in the John Foster West awards issue of *The Charlotte Poetry Review*.

"What If" and "When They Named Me" reprinted from *Prairie Schooner* by permission of the University of Nebraska Press. Copyright © 1992 University of Nebraska Press.

For their friendship and wise counsel, I thank Audrey Alenson and Lisa Sewell, who helped order these poems; many thanks also to E.J. Miller Laino, Nora Mitchell, and Ellen Watson for their guidance in shaping this manuscript; Ralph Black, Celia Bland, Pamela Sheingorn, Sasha Troyan, and Jean Valentine, whose support and encouragement sustain me; and Brian Murphy, grazer-beside.

CONTENTS

Cain, the image of God, gave the simple earth of the field a voice and a sorrow, and God Himself heard the voice, and grieved for the sorrow, so Cain was a creator, in the image of his Creator. God troubled the waters where He saw His face, and Cain became his children and their children and theirs, through a thousand generations, and all of them transients, and wherever they went everyone remembered that there had been a second creation, that the earth ran with blood and sang with sorrow. And let God purge this wicked sadness away with a flood, and let the waters recede to pools and ponds and ditches, and let every one of them mirror heaven. Still, they taste a bit of blood and hair.

— MARILYNNE ROBINSON, *Housekeeping*

GENERATION

The Sign

for M.B.G.

He says I have a history
and that he doesn't, not really. Not
like mine. All day he's filled
the cups of our friends
with more wine, the many glasses
trembling with their sour wash. I know
he means he was not in his body molded by
the blunt print of a father's foot, that he never
lay outside his parents' locked universe
for the span of a clear night. And yet,
the idea of the print still lingers on the underside
of his torso: the perfect curve of the heel; and
the sound of the latch possibly clanging
quietly echoes even now. Doesn't it? Does he not hear
the awful hasp whisk shut? — Why
do I want him to? But here
is the tuneful wine chiming in the glasses: I love
even the look of this drink, the pale gold
bits of fruits' skins
orbiting together in the glass, how they still hold
one summer's ferocious sun. My friend sits beside me —
from the window near us, I can see
the great tree in the rain as it begins:
first one leaf shudders, then several.
Then all the leaves stir, making similar motions.

The Gesture

When my brother says he wants to
step in front of a semi
and just get it over with —
no one wants him around anymore, anyway —
I start remembering the man who
lay himself down on the subway tracks
at Union Square, last summer, how he sprang down
lightly to the stretch of steel grids
that divides the long way of the city
into ladder-rung squares: *You can
do it, You can do it* and then he lay down and
folded his arms. It was the R train
that runs there. His skin looked gray
because the light is bad at that end of the platform,
there were only a few people,
someone called to him and he said
It's my life, all right? Then
someone cut the power, the large engines
paused, people jumped down and bent over him.
He had folded his hands on his stomach
and I remember him shaking his head,
and that when they helped him upstairs
one policewoman wearing a stiff fire-coat
had her hand on his shoulder, the way a parent might
hold a young boy crossing the street
not wanting to embarrass him by holding his hand.
The way, when the vet had said it was a brain tumor,
I cupped her front paws, which she had always liked,
I think it made her feel safer, and at the moment
of the injection she raised her head and looked back,
her lips drew back a little but she looked
over her shoulder — to take one last look
at the world. To bare one's teeth. To go
unwillingly.

On the afternoon after the brakes fail

I call in absent
from work and stay indoors,
doing housechores.
The mouth of the vacuum inhales
perfectly, a good machine,
and the plates in the drainboard
exhale steam that stuns the kitchen window. Outside,
an iron rain. Here, while the yeast proofs,
I play the television — I keep wanting voices that speak
when I need them to, boxed voices that hush
at the turn of a dial. Someone invested in terror
shouts *Freeze*; someone else
does. I lose count of the flour, cup enough in,
work the dough's flesh
for as long as necessary. On the public station
the Frugal Gourmet stains a plank with garlic;
his hands, 12 inches high, stroke the strung grain
of the wood for its lowest chord,
for the way the countertop hums against it.
The dough ropes and knots at my knuckles,
I punch back as I have learned, break
the glutinous filaments apart,
tear the tough proteins. The screen shows
a blender's rotary blades blurring under
a buzz, under a few words, *aspic, brine, saltpeter*. We cut
to a stockpot. Hands lift out soaked meat,
hold it to the lens: a tongue.
The pixels keep it a long time quivering. He says
it's a matter of history, that country people
have known to let nothing go
to waste. Well-advised, he says, a delicacy, the thumbs rolling
the milky peel of skin from that budded muscle,
with his nails paring the sinews from the untender roots

still intact, where the stump must join the throat in the lower jaw,
in the huge effort
of swallowing and speech. We don't see much of this
these days, he says, although in some quarters
a guard will cut out a prisoner's tongue
with equal economy, with gravity, even, since
if the knife slips
the wrong vein opens and the punishment turns
useless. I hate the perfect,
fine-honed tools, I fear men with steady hands, my own hands
which seldom waver — I sit there and tell the gray, sweet-faced man
he is a jerk, he's salting a recognizable body part,
I know he can't hear me, I know it's nuts
to address an object, but I want him to be interested
in what the torn tongue might say, lying
on the barracks floor, looking fish-like, familiar.
The one wavering on the screen
disappears behind a freezer door,
making the sounds of prayer.
The rain begins to interfere
with my set's reception. I shut it off,
I open the oven door, where
the bread is rising, I listen to it breathe.

What the Door Gives Onto

People in drugstores always look familiar:
it's the way the medicinal light washes
the spare features of browsers,
so that the glancing angle of a neck,
the planed lines of a hand
running over the swells
of aspirin bottles, these might mean
people you've lived with, or, like last night
on Twelfth Street, people you can imagine
life with, the way seeing how that woman by the shampoos
stood slumped in her bristling coat, you knew her
in her bathrobe, 5 a.m., watching the coffee brew.
Hinge of sleep, I should have said to her, there
at the conditioners, *lung ash proving mirrors,*
heart's nest to the man cradling a 2-liter cola, *heart's nest*
of cord and fur strands, but I left
for the line at the check-out counter, the earnest finger-drumming,
our communal impatience
for cough syrup and stomach remedies. How long, then,
could it have taken
me, caught at the last
in the doorway — someone leaning
in, heavily, carrying a headcold like a shoulderbag —
how long were we matching steps and
lunges, caught in that
speechless dance our bodies know
without us (quietly wanting all the body's failures to pass
unnoticed), and then, how slowly
did I spill the packages on the chipped steps
under the sodium glare? The man waiting there
for spare change, how did he know me
by that which fell from my hands, the bottles and combs,

the rims of his fingernails under the streetlamp,
the glazed ridges of flesh lining the night with signs,
how did he know when he said,
Mine, he said, *Leave it alone.*

Flight Delayed by Fog

for H.R., 1902–1990

After his stroke,
I knew he would not know me,
I stood in line for my boarding pass
and the face of a 707 looked through plate glass
to be just as blank as his would look and
while there was time to spare I saw also
how imprintable the face is, how I could imagine
curiosity in the deep-set headlamps, concern for passengers
shaping the nose, and how this might save me.
I saw the sheen on the surface
of his eyes and that his gums were going gray
and that when I pressed the fingers that lay outside
the bedsheet I was waiting
for his hand to close
over mine so that I would not be
alone. I held my hand up to the window because
a searchlight had lurched toward the terminal
and watched my hand turn
amber, living, strange. What
is there to know? When our plane
lifted it shook
off pavement, street signals, furthest reaches
of elms and commercial buildings,
it pitched over the stormfront
heavily, to rid itself of
its riders. The
body of the plane shook at the seams
and if it broke apart
we would spill out the way the contents
of an egg drop from the shell
and we would be gone. I saw this from the cabin window,
I sat in a group of people who were
strange to me and saw that we were all afraid.

The Labor

All I want to do now
is go back to that
instant, the windowlight throwing its broad arm
across his torso, the blanket curled
at our naked thighs, the bed itself
darkly gleaming like a mineral, a vein
of rich ore, that moment
I hit him
again, again,
if I could have broken him a little open,
struck the specific place between those two ribs
on his left side, that furrow which is
the missing rib, my gone origin,
God, then he might have loved me,
he would have said no cruel thing
meaning I too much desire
him — his attention, the sharp
black of the hairs on his face at their roots —

I keep looking at that woman, kneeling beside her lover,
the flash of her arms at their work, it felt so
good, to drive the heels of my hands
into that flesh, there was the force of my packed bones
and the thick earth of his body, which hardly gave
at all — for a moment I thought
I had finally become my mother
knocking apart the mortal
clay she'd made with her hands,
but it was still me, pounding frantically on the front door
from the inside of my life, too many locks, and my maker
heavily running toward me —

The cup

on the saucer makes a death-
rattle, ceramic sound of brokenness,
the sound of the rift
between two people, clink and crack
of the frangible heart
clattering against its protective envelope, the noise
of the saucer cursing the cup
is the sound I woke to
in the middle of that night before
I moved my grandmother to the
home, the harsh unbending
pottery was what I heard from my bed on the floor
of the stripped living room, dinnerware
smashing in the trash, 2 a.m. and she was cleaning
out her life, the things I'd begged her to keep for the new
room she was throwing away: to spite me,
to make sure she'd remember she had nothing
left, her husband dead, her child always
her child, and me
saving myself. Down the dark hallway I shouted
Enough, toward the lit kitchen I said You
horrible woman, How could you, You
must hate me, by then I was at the black
plastic sack, saying something about failure, and then I
looked her in the eyes — she looked so sad — and she
held out her cup and saucer before her and she said Sharon,
I'm making tea. And then she offered me some.

The Maker

At the service the rabbi
likens my grandfather to a pot: he was well-
made, the rabbi says, of good metal, re-
soundly tempered. He held
water, not like the other pots in the rabbi's anecdote
who despite themselves bear
hairline cracks, seepage — and it's true,
he is a thing now, the casket lays on its dais
locked from the inside, but was he all his life
a pot? I know he was
of gentle humor, his
sides untainted, but did he
preserve himself from sudden flame, did he tend to
his lining? He was bad at being a pot,
much as he tried — oh, let him be
an other thing, let him not be
what he was, that man
fixed in the old snapshot, bearing his girl on his back,
the plaster casts binding her malformed feet, his hands on them:
the father and the daughter
weigh each other down with
pity, fifty years he has
fed her and borne her
up and staggered under her
illnesses and not let go even as
the substance of his body
crumbled, I swear you can already see in both their
bodies the metal sour with disappointment — if this man is
a thing now then what
was he then, was he
a figure of the father, was he

the casted frame holding her up, little dollop, fifty years at the riverbank?
Was he the sculptor gazing, did he blush at
the cracks in his work, did he hide his eyes? Was God
that lonely, stirring the ashes and clay, did He
whisper when He called the mixture flesh
of His flesh, had He wept yet?

The Coroner's Assistant

When I look at my mother's dead body
I see bright light that bathes it, the staring
steel table a kind of convex bathinet,
and my mother's limbs are
swollen, flesh drops off the bone
at a touch, like soup meat, because the body
slumped four days unfound under the shower. They're trying to find
my mother's cause of death. The coroner
runs her knife lightly down my mother's core,
folds one breast back, the other, the skin
furls its bodily wings. The inside of my mother.
Would it be pink? Rot-black? The coroner
in her kindness names my mother's organs: the contents
of the liver is a bit of yellow bile, the bladder
weighs 90 grams, the good lungs which lack their spirit, the knife
slides underneath, severs certain cords, she lifts
the womb, which is empty, and pliant, and un-
marked. Each of my mother's parts
drops into a tub of water,
each makes its small splash-sound of dis-
placement as it goes under. Meanwhile,
and there was a meanwhile, and much loud bone-sawing,
and probably a lunch break, the coroner has found
the source of death, the heart of my mother
is broken. Over and over, I step forward
and say, I did it, I wasn't there. She
fingers the heart, that sweet sea animal, its many valves,
the collapse in its wall. But it was
a young heart. But it was tormented. But
what was the torment. But there was a torment.

My mother's body lays there, splayed, flayed,
the wound in her trunk is her trunk,
but my mother's body is not
my mother, I could burrow in those plushy unfolds and not
touch her. This is why my mother died: she lived un-
reached, which
killed her, the death throes wrenched her spirit out
through her eyes, her skin's multiple pores — I saw that departure
happen, many nights, I thought she was slamming my body
     on the floor
and holding it and slamming it
out of her excess life, but really I was witnessing
the exit of her, that writhing. Poor coroner! she does not think
to cradle my mother's contents, she does not whisper to the
vacant soul-place, but heaps the pieces in, sprung
springs of a clock. Does God wear gloves
to dismantle a soul? Has God little to say
at the end of the day's work, is the last sound in that room
the gurney set into the drawer, the drawer's
liquid clasp clapped shut? Does the unclaimed soul
heavily curl in the freezer? What happens when they can't find
that soul's next of kin, whose heart do they bury it in?

A Pardon

And I take back the canary, my
mother's canary, named Martin
for K-Mart, who sang as he was
intended, Martin of the full notes and the fatted
breast, neither being enough to
protect him from me in my
eighth year, Martin, kept in a wire cage
in the spare room. I could say the truth
to no one else, I understand this
now, I would poke with a pencil the underside, for
the crash of wings and vertebrae at the bars,
I pulled feathers, choice tail feathers, down that signified
helplessness, the torso's bristly feathers of defense, I plucked them out,
it was a glut, a binge, the throaty squawks and the frantic
beating of bones on the wire, I wanted
that, I knew that
was wrong, but it felt
better only then. I could see how
it looked, how it must have looked
like I was flapping my body, the way they shook
me, the shoulders, the head, elbows,
the spine and the thighs slamming
in place on the floor. And Martin,
I wanted him to know
we were together in it,
there's no way out, I'd tell him,
and then he'd know I knew
more. What else was left me?
I didn't know then I wanted them
in that cage, in that same
panic of blood they had given

me. And when it was over,
when I unlatched the wire door
and held the fantastically small
body, felt the thready heart, saw
the beak move numbly,
when I'd take him in my hand to take the hand away
as if to take back the act
that hands have done, I was asking
his pardon, he who allowed me
my single power, who showed
how I lived then, how to live.

The Relic

I don't know what matters now
I have stood in the morgue and run my hands over him,
his dead body beading in the thaw,
now I have thumbed my grandfather's lashes and
shorn the fatted curls at his nape to
keep something. I cannot. It's a mistake,
isn't it, to want something from the ones I love —
even if they weren't suffering under my love they were
suffering, I heard him that last day cry out trying to speak
but it was not the pain from not speaking,
he had nothing to say to me, and I've seen my mother
rip the air running at me, I have fled her and turned to see
her teeth flash in the hall,
I've stood luckless in the narrow bathroom
and with the thrumming globes of my shoulder-sockets
and the ungiving porcelain sink I have
braced the door shut, I have heard her
back up the few paces and
calculate, heard the gaze move over the door and then
the pounding step the angle the full
body ramming the door, I have soaked up with my ribs
and the long pliant stem of my spine the frantic
wood door, she groaned and
wept for what was hers. What was hers. — Well, wasn't I? Didn't I give
in, tell her I loved her even as I watched
the door in the mirror — and when I caught sight of the face
mirrored against the door, a framed face, that I told
It doesn't matter, it doesn't matter — was I
nothing, then? And what am I now that I've stood at his shut
casket, not having

seen her thirteen years and then seeing her
the fatherless, the lifeless eyes — it isn't that she does
not love me, it's that she's not there. Now I see it,
we're not-bodies, bodies of not, we are
not. But
that can't be — even not
having her, even not having him, haven't I
stood with the sighing surgical shears
and then the spade of red earth and
just now, writing this: I still want
to want — I have kept that door shut till my bones
cried, that door
hammering like a human heart.

Paradise

Sometimes in the car we'd sing Hey there,
Georgy girl, why do all the boys
just pass you by, we would pass under cloud banks
that are the source of the first world

and my mother, plotting ways to Get Rich
Without Working, would turn to me
and promise I'd never leave her,
I was her best friend, we were practically

married, she'd get rid of the worm
my father and then we'd be
always together. My mother's hands
were shapely wings moving, my mother's eyes
changed color in the sun. It's true

she used me as a look-out when she stole from stores, and
even then she talked to herself outside,
and, later that afternoon, she'd turn
to me, still not rich, still
unrecognized, curse my birth and

clutch her thighs that could not just once re-
vert the order of this world and undo me,
draw me back up the seethy channel
to my two unknitted parts and ah my mama
lay upon me shouting to whom and massively
slammed me on the floor — but she was

a god driving me out of Eden,
of course I loved her, but imperfectly —
later she'd kneel and ask me to hold her
and she was flesh and hair

and bone and ash chuff
knocking slightly in my arms

this summer, in her steel canister, under streaming light —

I abandoned my maker
half my life ago. I have been banished forever.

What If

What if I really loved them
when they were savage, when he
leapt across the room to me
and threw me into the wall,
my back slapped the sheer
face like dough slaps against its maker's
palm, maybe I
loved it when she blew into a
rage at my slow chewing, ponderous
work at the table, the table rose
in her hands as if she were an anti-
medium hauling the forces from the antiworld
into ours — I must have loved it, I had their
full attention, they fought me like wild
animals fight with one paw in the steel mouth, bare
thrashing at the trapper,
gleam of the pelt and bared
hate beaming from their eyes — I
lived for it, I lived
against it, I was always waiting for it
to happen. When I sat at my
desk in school I'd think about what they were
going to do, I devoted myself to
the study of them, the charts on the wall of
health class showed
her fallopian tubes, his intricate
vas deferens, the vast
entrails and the 7 layers of skin were
their large animal bodies, staunch legs and
abdomens, sturdy mammals

forcing me to kneel before them at night.
Maybe what I loved was
having to beg
to live, I kissed their ankles when they told me
so they'd give me supper, a roof
over my head, I saw so clearly
how small I was at their feet, how low I could crawl, how desperate
to live, and when I
cast my eyes up to
the roof they made bending over me I saw
how desperate they were,
because I was learning geometry, too, the pure
face of the roof's surface
and the infinite line
it pointed to.

Penance

O that thou shouldst give dust a tongue
To crie to thee,
And then not heare it crying!
—GEORGE HERBERT, "DENIALL"

First, she would lie crosswise
on my bed reaching
down as if we were in a life-
boat drill where the mother must save
the daughter from drowning, our thick
screams so that someone might
rescue us, her hands
catching my shoulders, slick of hair, neck
twisting, if there had been water
and no floor, a fragment of raft
in place of the bed, if she were calling
Hold on, I would have believed it
was the desperate nature of love, neither of us able
to leave the other alone in that soaking
cold, but she was shouting Let go and
I would not do that, I held to
the wooden frame of the bed, twined my
feet in the slats, skull drumming
on the planks beneath and above me
shouting I could not make out
over the pound and thrum — deep under the bed
I knew there was the clouded pool to drop down in, the wash
of sleep, suck and pull, she held me there at its
outer lip, was she lowering me in,
hauling me up, outside the bed we
were a stain on the air, we beat up and down
in a blur, as a single
string is plucked and quivers, sings

furiously, until no hearing was left us,
every sound flew
asunder, intended elsewhere. Did she
hear us? I looked hard as I could into
her eyes, which were radiant, always
radiant, and under the watery surface,
where light entered her —
I wanted a sign, I wanted some scar to explain it, an
agony on the flat disc of her iris — not
to find my face there.

The Scar

Afterwards, I looked out
from inside my body, I saw
the outline of it
was the shape of my life, too,
my form puckering at the nipples,
where I want to give forth,
and joined into the bright humming corner
where I most crave to be reached —
of course that place wears its hood,
I could see how I want things
and pretend not to. He was laying heavily
on me, resting that dense torso on mine,
the way an island leans
into a hidden tectonic plate — clearly I am
a piece of planet, damp and furrowed — and between me
and him a portion of that primeval ooze substance
which still remembers the taste of lightning
crept, as a river trickles far from its delta. And then
I felt my many-parted hair
dividing, I felt my ribs
open like a hand — it wasn't that I was crying,
it was a huge rending of my structure:
I want to be inside
him. I almost hate that his body seals itself
against me. And unseals me,
and blessedly fills me, as a plant is filled
with its milky quick.
And then draws from me that core; then that slaying emptiness
again. But,
later, this body of his will shred will molder;
my own strong arms will crumple and dissolve.
So maybe what matters

is that red crescent mark
I left on his clavicle, by holding on too hard
or trying to not cry out. I know it will fade,
but also it won't fade, he'll live out his life
with my sign deeply embedded in him, one of the many arcs
that make up the body: the shape of lifting
bounded at the beginning-
and the end-points. Maybe this is the true shape
of the human life. And all the time
he was saying, I've got you, I've got you,
and I was wishing that were so.

At the open-air cafe a friend

asks me why I write poems. While he says this,
he's eating a hamburger, flesh
carved from the cow's side, and
riced along the inherent grain of
the creature's lifespan, and fried
so that that cow's steaming blood
enters into the veins of the earth's air
which are the thin currents of wind
we breathe in. I can't say a thing
because breath has taken me over
the edge of my memory. Why

do I write this? Why do I love
to see the excellent teeth at their work?
What kept me struck dumb
ripping open the yeasty roll
for an answer, for the roll's un-
ravelling into its separate components.
I shook my head because I wanted
to lay my head on the table and moan but I didn't
know him that well, only enough to say

I don't know. Not enough
to say As a child I thought I would
die, every night. To say When my body
hit the wall when my head hit the floor my
back hit the edge of the stair the fist
my skull the fist my side the grip my throat
I became a gasp, a heart beat, a
stop. So that now I am a breach, I am my body without
breathing that desperately pries open the next
breath and cries out in gratitude at the breath and
cries out in loathing of the cry and cries out
and cries out

Rubbing My Father's Back

That was when
I began to learn
what I would need to know. It would happen
on those Saturdays, in the afternoon, there was always
the ball game on tv, the half-eaten
plate of Skippy and Welch's jelly
sandwiches. He would lie face pressed
to the nubby couch, I would go to him,
I would set hands to his body, lifting the thick shoulder blades
in their slick skin, creasing the gnarled column of neck, I would pry
at the place where his neck and skull hinged
shut, I would draw up the wings of flesh at his ribcage.
He said nothing during this, I was easing him
toward sleep, the announcer, crying the game,
had faded, my father and I
intent on finding
what felt good to him, I could feel
the halves of my own back stretch,
when the ropy shoulders uncoiled, I
felt them let go, I felt the sap run in my own arms,
I practiced this, I see now I had to, pressing the
sweet grease of his forearms, unclenching
the fists that had split open the skin of my torso and
knocked open also portions of scalp I could not see
even in mirrors. I knew he would do this
again, so I held the hands open, the fingers
waving in the air, like antennae probing the emptiness, and then
I had put him to sleep,
the hands lay quiet, brown as cracked walnuts,
the tenderness of them, holding their lives in
their skin, away from me, I learned then
how to love them.

My Mother Bathing

After a fight she would want me
everywhere: I would sit with her while she
skinned chicken for supper, in the evening
she would hold her hands out for me
to file the nails down,
when she bathed I kept
her company. It must have been a kind of atonement for her —
the way, naked, the flanks shook, the flesh
collapsed and folded, it was as if the massiveness of her
had left, as if she had taken it off — I knew
she would hate my looking later, but after her thighs
had clamped my thighs, after her nails
had slit the undetectable skin on my ribs, after her arms
had driven me into the floorboards, raised me up
to themselves, pressed me back down, after her body
had done all it could
to my body, she wanted me
to see hers was ordinary, soft, a little
pasty except for the brick-brown
sexual places, and it flinched from
the scald of the tap just as my own body would,
she would flush under the steam and
stroke her body with the soap,
and the motions her hands made on the length of her arms,
how graceful they were. Then
she'd give me the bar,
it looked shock-white,
the size of a finch and slippery,
making rapid movements as I held it,
I guided it in stripes and arcs over the curved back, past

the beaded shoulder blades, close as I could to the
mild nape of her neck,
when I did well, my hands moved as her hands had,
lovely leaving their trail of lather,
I saw how she bent forward
under my hands, how the head sagged, as if
all along, what she'd needed was
to be made clean to be forgiven.

Afterlife

I last laid eyes on her
the day I moved her in
to the Old People's Home, where she could
live out the rest of her twenty-three days,
I propped her spare cane against
the single bed, and then
the second bell rang, like recess,
but lunchtime. The Director led her away
too soon, I only had time to quickly kiss her,
not to stroke her hair, not to tell her goodbye
fully; she walked down the light-filled hall
holding onto the wall as though grasping
a railing, or a ladder rung
after rung, her purse dangling from her forearm
and the Director steadily steering her
by her left elbow, the way you lead a child
to the Principal's office — it was such a
long walk, it took time the way a car accident takes
time, watching the windshield blossom into
its original structure. When she turned
the corner, she cried to those assembled there, *You're all
so beautiful!* I could have
killed her when I heard that, but she probably still thinks
she meant it, wherever she is, though she's no-
where, except in me, vestigially (her good, strong hair, her
impermeable teeth), though she only wanted
that they like her. That she might please them.
Really, my bubby was addressing the invisible
angelic host, all those fierce wings rustled
at the glowing table — it was a lie she needed to
tell herself. And who am I

to talk, I come from a people who fashioned
an animal out of metals that they might
take comfort. They were lost
in the limitless sands. The great Hand guiding them
by their napes had faltered and withdrawn. Have
pity on them. And me, with my lies: I still
need him to come in my mouth, even
though he does not love me, even though
this is the age of plague — at my table
there has to be a little death mixed in
with the taste of salt, a little
threatened loss, at my feast I have to have
the char and ashes with the roast —
Maybe they *were* beautiful, those haggard folk
in their bathrobes and crumbling faces. That fold
at the non-pedestal base of his
sex, which joins the groin and thigh, permanently babyfatty,
where the tough black hairs grow thinner, almost
mild: Such a sweet desert. Such a gentle exile.

Transgressor

As though it were happening again, the new cat
plunges her fang into the succulent meat of my hand,
she has to she
has to she
cannot get her tooth out
of my palm, I think she must like it —
no, she accedes to the will of the species.
As though it might help her, to puncture the live-
ly sinews of my hand. And yet, she flinches.
She thinks she will be
hit. And this is when
I see in the furred body
the foot which is the tooth
in my side, the leather-shod thorn
that bites me in my midsection, bi-
sects me into body and
body, soul gone out-
side as the child goes forth from the two parents
to live among others of the tribe, and where the soul was
is a blank cleft, a furrow that joins two ribs
where the foot in its tanned hide
buries itself, but
not buries, plants itself, because
the foot is of the man
who forgets, who kicks to lift the flesh
up from its hiding place, his daughter
has said no, she had not made the bed, and who is she
to say no, is he not the father, what is he, what
is he, he kicks to dis-
cover what he is, his foot a solid
thing, his leg a material
force, the man who fears his daughter
will erase him with her *no*, her will

somehow what the boy he was wept under
under the belt that tore the air with its grinning buckle
and then its biting prong
that ate the fabric of his body. Until he is
rent cloth, and seed, and he wants to be re-
made, whole and so terrible
the father's hand will drop the belt and tremble.
The foot that planted itself in me to find him took
root in my ribcage, fallow soil of my gone soul
dense with the haired stalks of my father's
terror. I almost I almost I almost
love what my father did to me, the minor beatings,
the way the pains from the foot radiated through my bloodstream,
and that the tooth of the pain,
the branched plant of pain, takes
its place in my body, which is the garden
of unnamed things. Finds some relief there.

The Traveler

When I got the call that they were
carrying her into the ambulance, her heart
going, not going, I got to the airport
in minutes, and then from the northeast to the midwest I sat
clawing the seat arm because I wanted her
to stay alive, and this
was a way of praying. I've always felt
it was the only kind of prayer I could do, clench my hand and
think *Please don't, Please don't.* By the time I
got to the hospital
to see that grey, creamy face,
the bluish eyelids flickering over the breath-mask, each breath
full of the body's brine,
I was thinking about love: was there any inside me, was there any
love within my grandmother — But what
do I know about love. I stood at the bars
of her bed, the room was
brownish-dark, workers moving down the hall, serum dripping
down a clear tube, her eyelids shuddering, I couldn't
hold her hand because
of the cords, so I stroked the length of her wrist-
bone, I traced the channel of her blood because
what else is there, there was just the narrow ply of skin
which is the divider, just the bright globules of fat
hardened like mistakes, and the organs bobbing in the thick
ocean — she was not resting she was
tiring, failing swimmer in the channel between continents,
in trouble, in the brunt of the elements — when suddenly she
opened her eyes I think she finally
saw it, the ocean, the wan body ridden upon it, that moment
she opened her eyes I think she saw
she was alone. So I stopped

pressing my hand upon hers, running my fingers over her
skin — I could not change
the force of the current, and that
she would have to let it bear her away.

The Message of My Grandmother's Death

The night she died
I heard it but I could not see
how she could do that, I
turned in the room as a stone
turns in a palm, in locked woe,
I walked my four rooms because I could not
stand holding that ache in my arms,
my very sockets wrenched
empty. And then I walked un-
looking smack into the open
door with the side of my head
as if my body had stepped into the other side
to carry her back
but failed. I cannot transcend
the effect of impact, which is
what dying must be, that daze from a blow to the head. When my mother
would straddle me and knock my head on the floor — stubborn jar
she had to open — and then
be done,
I'd feel dazed like that
at what the light looked like, at the pain not
pain because it had crossed over
to rhythm, at sounds re-
turning, which grew loud: my breath. How
did I not dissolve, how was I still
an object in the world — I didn't get it, the space between
my skull ridges sore, a tooth-pit sprouting blood,
I was the space between, myself. So lonely, the body
trying to leave. I think I was meant to become
a film of sweat, a sneer, a *fuck-you*.
Sometimes when my mother had got tired and gone

my panting took on
meaning — as a novice takes on vows, white robes placed on
the bowed back, the sheet I lifted from her bruise-smeared corpse —
the first, ancient chant; the living song.

The Girls' Home

Back then I knew I was dreamed
because one of these Sundays I was going
to disappear, they said I would, and
that would prove my whole life had never
happened. They would drive me to the Girls' Home,
I would hold my breath in the back seat,
his college suitcase was jammed under my feet
and I would lay a forefinger on it
the way you make a sign
on someone's lips to shush them. Then
he would pull over
and say *See? See?* It was like a castle,
someone had taken a burnt sienna
crayon to the gables and turrets, the place was full
of calm, I thought then, full of girls who had been
dreamed and disappeared. I remember the
prong of the car door, how I dared myself to
pull it open and run, up the lawn to
the elm overlooking the Home, they would blink and I'd have
vanished, first
up the lower branch broken down by wind,
then the chewy trunk itself, then the leafblack
confusion of shadow. After I disappeared,
I could hear the buzz of crickets under
their voices, as the car pulled away, they were
a man and woman bright in the front seat. I saw how,
from far away, they'd look blue and thin in the
house where they had me
pressed face down on the carpet, where they twisted
the joints of my body to the places the limbs could not turn to, one

curled a shoulder, the other took a hip so that I must have looked
like a person climbing inside out,
a prisoner they held for questioning, *What*
are you going to do now? What are you going to do
now?

When They Named Me

Long ago, deep in the family
body, there was the name
Aron, plighted word of the
man with the rod in his
left hand to summon plague with, desperate
phonemes leaping onto the land, aa
rone, bitter liquid syllable my mother
came here with,
grief sound I made in my
throat when I
found out I loved her. And all through the long
bones of his people my father
had his name, Kraus, lanky
on the chromosomes just before they
dance and divorce, it was there in him,
Kraus, first the jaw clench, the molar
churn, when I say it too slow I could
weep, then the savage opening, the wild
groan, *ow*,
ow, naked begging I would make when her bright
teeth lodged in my wrist, *ow God it
hurts*, and then *ssss* —
they knew what they'd make when they
made me, when they
met on their blind date in the bowling alley he
looked at her open face in the sharp light, the puzzled
curve of her eyelid, the poor mouth saying oh,
she looked at his blunted chin and his scarred forehead that
understood some things — shy of
holding hands and yet they looked at
each other outside the 4-Star Lanes on Kedzie and
saw what they were born for, the 2 shapes

their mouths made, ohn and ow, their bodies
born to carry the pain-verbs
toward each other, so that
months later when they switched off the lamp and
rode into the slick banks of their sex their words
mixed in the wind, the very vowels coupled, the
grief-vowel and the rage-vowel
fitted inside one another. Sometimes I
want to think they howled the night they made me, did
one of them cry out? Did the
other try to gentle, did the other say Shhh, shhhh?

The Fence

A week after the visit
he sent me a letter
that he was sorry, he couldn't help
needing to be alone, he had to
not see me again. He hoped
I would understand. The postmark
was the day I had held
my grandfather's dead body, the seal
bearing the date denoted the after-
noon, so I was signing papers
at the chapel when he slid the letter in the one-
way box. And I understood: we
are so alone — holding him in my arms
means I will have to again
let go, that crushing weight-
lessness like a wind I have to
walk into. This is the wind
streaming at his turned back,
carrying spores and ash that I taste,
that mix in my former lover's hair. From miles away
he later sent me a gift, that we might
be friends, a snapshot of the beautiful fence
between us, which marks our
opposite courses, and cannot stop the wind.

Loving My Mother

When my mother died
I think my own heart
cracked a little; but
not from her death: it was
the finding out that she was dead,
it was the sitting on the kitchen
floor, it was the thick square of answering machine
that I raised and lowered
almost to the floor — almost the smashing
in my mother's grip of me — it was
the struck thud of the wall on my head,
and inside the wall my mother
in the drawer, on a tray, on a conveyor
shelf, like a big Dunkin' Donut in the morgue,
twenty weeks thickly curling, the face
so long shredded, swervy with
swarming mold, the big thighs
partly dissolved. Of course my mother's mind
shredded years before, broke its own trail
on its way out, and left the two lobes of her
self dis-
juncted, the loving half and the hating half
tumbling with an hourglass sand-rumple, the before and after
of my mother's nature
turning with the up and down motions
she made clasping me to and fro
her. It wasn't until
days later, when I'd risen
from my floor and its walls that sturdily
spring up from it, risen and gone to the heart
of the continent, that I found myself standing

on the graveyard grass,
holding my mother. Finally
she could be the heartbroken child,
infant, even, in her shiny canister
I could comfort her, rock
and sing to her, put my arms fully around her
knocking shards, her massive dust, tuck her into her
square bed in the humming planet. How good
my mother's death, how good my mother
to me, letting me
soothe her, and quiet her, and satisfy her.

What I Could Not Save

Because when we took in the stray pup
      named Lucky, my father would
      kick her so that the foot
      would shape the body, the silky
      fur draping over the lustrous shoe
      the way a burnishing cloth would
      polish a hammer, because he meant
      to teach her, the whistly shrieks too
      long in stopping, a tactical error, a
      weakness, I thought, if she indulged now, she
      wouldn't last, because when she turned
      mean, I understood
      it was a kindness to gas her,

because in the locked room, I lay
      by the corduroy slippers and said
      nothing, I watched his crossed feet
      tap, each tapped the other to test its
      own solidity, because I could think of
      nothing worth saying,

I knew when I saw the boy who would be
      my father's new child, whose flesh
      stretched like a drum skin over his
      bones so that anyone might see
      the chalky grain of his skull, the blue veins
      ticking like thought, the fine
      work of his jaw, I knew when
      he asked what *for your own good* means, I knew
      I would not tell him, that I would leave
      without telling him
      what I knew, that nowhere in the things
      he had of mine was it yet written,
      Save yourself, you must save yourself.

Making Dinner, Thursday Night

I was pouring beans into a pot, black beans
purple like roe, each one clattered
against the vessel's metal sides, an odor
rising, sweet, meaty smell,
and finally I stopped hating, just for a moment,
I held them in handfuls
to the tap, sorting for stones,
frijoles negros, turtle beans, their ovate denseness, their
mineral glow, the frond
that had ripened, sent up sap,
feeding these bean-fruits until they were ready to drop down —

                                                          It's not
that I'm one of the toothy plants vibrating in the sun —
the rich pods' swell and burst
that I'd give anything to stop, arrest, halt, cease, just for a while
until I'm ready — it's that I could be ready,
it's that I'm really in the kitchen with that other kitchen
slowly falling away, the dust rising to the water's skin
which I pour off, replace with fresh water,
it's that I'm weeping over a pot of beans —
not for my own life, so long I have been the reeling daughter
that I may never dare motherhood — it's my own children
I weep for, how long they've waited, how patiently,
how much they crave sun, rain, a taste of the wind.

The Dazzle

My friend's baby turned over in her crib,
today, in the summer midday
wash of light. There was a small whirl of dust motes
rainbowing; maybe she wanted to go on looking,
or to whirl, herself. Maybe she wanted a rest
from the dazzle of human life. The crib slats
cast almond shadows on her rectangular sleep, and
we stood there, the new mother and I,
sentries at the border of her
dream life. Which is her life, I think: first the desire
to gaze, or touch, or turn away; then the difficult decision
to act, the body of desire.

                    But maybe I just
want to think this, that there's a decision
to be made, a *yes* that happens in us, and then the assent,
which radiates outward. Sometimes his cock moves inside me
off center, it's like he's reaching toward my vital organs —
my vestigial appendix, my pulsing heart — so that I'm no longer
halved, and I can feel him taking us over the sill.
It's that kind of *yes* I mean. But the truth is, I'm scared
of that *yes* in me: when I took his narrow face in my hands
last night, his rough cheeks chafing my wrists,
I couldn't help it — it's that I didn't decide,
I didn't choose to say I love him, it happened in me,
the way there are elements that reel and collide and
collapse upon each other and produce something,
heat, radiance, in such abundance
the universe brightens, and we can't help it,
it's so fierce we have to avert our eyes.

The First Morning with Him

Light limns the sheets, there's
a glaze of it shaping our skins; it's that
forceful sort of light that pains me, the kind
I love to look into so that I can weep
as it reaches my interior. But now, not yet weeping,
I have my eyes mostly shut
with kissing, that veiled privacy. There's something about kissing
so almost lonely, the way it requires the
impermanent dark, the heavy
turn inward, no matter how close I try to get
to him I'm fixed
here, in this body, drifting in its specific historical seas,

until I give the kiss up — when? — and
see him. His whole mouth opened, his broad tongue
creasing my breast, the long, aching minutes go
on, so finally I can
look at him: his jaw working, his eyes shut,
the lines at his throat giving off sun —

that he's alone, too. That he takes of the breast

as though it were food, some other life
in him coming awake; within the etched face of this man
is that first moment, that
original moment, when he was
entirely held, and rocked, and solaced,
before anyone left him.

                    This was the sixth day.
Then we rose up and went
into the stippled world. I did not say Who
are you, I did not say My dear one, I walked home and looked
at that woman, her
youth, her fine bones and reddening hair, her
moving among the rooms, — blithe,
tuneless hum — laying him in the cradle. Shutting the door.

Geniture

Rebecca Aron, who floated here in a big boat, when she was 16, to
join her beloved, who spoke to me in Russian and Yiddish and with
her gnarled fingers clenched me, by the skull, the ribcage—an anti-hug,
a charge, the information I need for this life packed in her carpal
bones, her fierce grip, her hair white on the pillow.

Sometimes I would wake at night and hear my father tapping the
adding machine, the pressure of numbers building up, like evidence,
enough information about my beloved and I'll have to leave him or
surely he'll leave me, the plastic keys clacking at his touch, some, and
more, and then the machine bursting open.

There weren't any voices there. No. Not true. But they were
shouting, the same voices, a similar shouting; not even shouting,
more of a call, a very satisfying call from deep in the torso. And
outside, the slap of wings, a wing thudding its hollow body. To burst
open, or to burst into the open; maybe they wanted that but it
terrifies me, all that blue.

I do far too much clutching. I should love the blue.

There was the steady pulse of the pyrex coffee percolator. Its happy
choke, its fulfilled gurgle and release. It's me who wants to hear
"happy" there. The way my mother, snoring, would not snore but
hum — out, out — as though singing to herself to keep asleep. If I
hear the percolator chortling I can keep asleep. The regularity of it,
that's what I love. The fear of the blue and the gazing at the blue.

And this morning, his fingers on my spine — sturdy, enclosing grasp
— every knot in my musculature might be a key, a percussive note:
maybe I am an instrument, a humming string or a gasping pot. If I
keep my eyes shut I could hear every repeated cry, the history of
them, they would continue; I would.

Wish-Shopping

Lemon pie, cupcakes, nonpareil icing,
torte. Wholegrain bread, sweet rolls,
cans of breadcrumbs, croutons to carpet
the floor of the cart. Cans of beets, cans
of applesauce, sugared milk, creamed corn,
both of us wheeling furiously, her cart
filling with items still out of my reach —
imported vinegars, boxed after-
dinner mints, bloody mary
mixers — while my cart would take on
an order, sometimes the blowzy look: a heap of oyster cracker
and tootsie roll packages
as an informal bed for the red jam jars, or
a stateliness: the cornerstone of saltines
holding up the house of Cheerios, the carts heavier,
we would move more slowly, as was our plan, approaching
the crucial aisle, the flesh bound in plastic and blood,
drumsticks, their gluey skins primed for the flames,
rump roasts I held in my arms, breasts of turkeys, chops
I could never match to a body. Further on, just past the
refrigerated section, the freezers of chocolate twirl cartons,
banana boats, neapolitan extravaganza, we limped, we heaved,
we barreled, we fought the power of floor wax. Then
we would roll, creaking,
behind the battery display,
every grocery has a battery display before the registers,
where we'd leave our paired carts, our masterworks,
our imperishable wants, they'd lean and
list against each other, full
and spoiling.

The Visit

When he held the bread up
and tore it into its four parts,
the crumbs colliding on the plate, when he
enclosed with his hands the cup
and named it, and gave us the morsels
of bread, naming them also,
and then when we were finished
carefully poured the remnant of crumbs
into the dregs of the cup and consumed
the leftover god portion
not out of greed but rightfully, taking what belonged
to him, truly, I wanted to weep —

                                        Oh, I've
wanted a God for this life, so
often I have envied the faithful. But
that moment what I thought was,
He's like me! My friend the priest he too
desires to transform his Maker, to take the Creator
in his mouth. I felt so grateful when I saw him
take those last pieces for himself
and swallow, swallow. It took a long time

for the other thought to come, one morning over coffee:
I hadn't wanted to weep; I had *tried* to.
All my life I am making
the shapes of trees, the sweep of hands
reveal my own empty arms. And what I want
to want is to be like
him, turning the coffee into sediment
and wine, forming the bread into a loving body,
changing my Maker into sustenance, and grace.

That Which Is Palpable

Since then, nothing's
happened. I have not woken
to a woman's teeth on my throat
or a man's finger probing my chest
to find that I am still
breathing. Whatever that woman and
that man found, I knew
they were deceived and that they loved
to deceive themselves with the body
of their making — when she chewed my
stringy veins, when he
palmed my next breath, it was
to take and to eat, really,
they thought they had me but they were wrong
and wrong, it was their own bodies they found there,
how they had to
feel each hand closing, each mouth.
That which is palpable, friend,
don't mistake it. My hand, here,
on your hand, this means nothing. That
I have placed it there
is all.

Finally

What I want is to break all the windows of my apartment
by throwing plates through them,
I want to hear some good cracks, I want
long, fine shards glossing the street
and blood on my hands, I want to
drive all the way back staining the steering wheel,
it will be light all 26 hours and the house
will still be there
and I'll have had foresight, extra plates
in the back seat, and my mother
will be in her canister but in the backyard
and buried just a foot underneath
and light rain on the ground, a stick in the dirt
pries her up —
I want just to handle the canister, try its
heft again, the small cries of the bone chips —
not to pry open and sift over ah no leave a few lids
clamped tight and my father
shall loiter nearby,
the fetid deaths of his skin cells un-
washed off, he so loves this dying, he still won't be
speaking but he will desire to speak,
his face will work at it
and the rain will work on his body
there will be much hissing in the world
this day, flakes of dead flesh and ash scraps
will rise up and rain back and
collect in gutter dreck and stream into
the water supply channel and the absolute smallest
particles of my parents will join the particles of other people
in the reservoir and they will be ladled up,
they will give baths, they will quench thirsts.

The Caretaker

Once my mother died I was also freed. Someone else
might love me, and my mother
wouldn't be there to show
what I really am: grizzled
daughter of the Other, hater
of the Other. And yet, an other Other
made me. The story goes,
she was a night nurse who took care of me
my first two weeks in the peopled region,
until the evening my mother found her
pinching my infant cunt lips as she diapered me,
when my mother, my righteous protectress,
banished her, and kept me for herself.
Was I crying, that night, did the index finger
hushing the flow I made pain me,
lance in the pith of the sexed infant? Was that
my first share of bliss, God in the Other
bringing me to the flat edge of the world,
rubbing me against the starry night of my new
body? Was Nurse Annie Saint Anne in '61
fondling the baby to prove ah the body unfolds it
widens and wets. Oh, Annie. I have wished
you were my mother. Now that she's dead,
I look for you in public
places, in the street, at the park,
I watch the wheeled babies and the toddlers
and I see you might be
a dark brown black woman, or maybe
lighter than my father, dark Jew triple Other,
and that my mother feared you.
As she feared her

self. Maybe she stood at her life's doorframe
one instant and doubted she could mother,
and later, at the sill, slipped the doubt
into the pocket of the Other's white uniform.
I'm glad she feared you, which means
she did not know you, and that at the beginning
of my life I was met by a dark, feared woman
who also stood slightly outside,
who may have been hated as I have been
ravenously hated, who may have hated
back, who therefore knows those whorls:
hate, hating back; the flesh
which is not the I but which,
when it comes to it, is all
I; the coming which is al-
most not flesh because so
other, so much among all others it is
where all I's are I's; the galactic pre-
dawn night marked
by stellar orbits in Another's thumbprint —
as your thumb printed the nub of me
with the signs of the next world,
and of our world.

The Address

The truth is, I worry
about when you'll die. I can't quite
let myself think I'll be there, but I want to think
someone will touch you then. There will be a bird
singing outside, I'm sure, the one I woke you up to hear:
three notes, in a minor key, the question mark at the end
of its phrase, but whether
you'll hear it . . . I know I should
not think this. Meanwhile
there are patches of mud, and my tree, which is
my tree, is starting
to leaf. And a man cycling up the sidewalk
hikes his tee shirt to his shoulders,
so that the moist skin of his back
streams forward, all of him bending
over the front wheel, the flesh taking in light
and giving back light. You
were making coffee for me. You didn't see this man,
but I wanted you to, which is a good thing. And
I looked up and you were holding the coffee pot,
setting down a mug, the coffee steam
lifted: that nut meat, toasted smell. There's too much
I don't say. It's such work to
not say When will you die. I dreamed I was writing
in a dark room, I couldn't see
the page, so I didn't know what
the words were, though I knew they would
matter. I kept trying to press my face
closer to the page; if I could make out the meaning,

I could take that other world
back into ours. The ink was thick black on the heavy sheet,
the pores soaking up ink, so that every letter
had a negative halo. And then pushing away
to read the whole, which was the pushing at you,
just before the bird, this morning, 4 a.m. Which was
the telling you, *I can't see it, I can't see it.* And you
covered my head with your palm.

To the Day

Six months after my grandmother died
I crossed 14th Street and a woman called me — Miss,
Miss — I had been looking at the broad, gouged intersection,
the rubble they'd brought up
out of the earth
where the pavement had buckled,
under the twilit snow
they were bringing the impacted masses out
to allow the wound to close, and it was six months,
I was sick of feeling I have no one left, all gone, all
gone, spoon gleaming to the bowl, sick of wondering
what she'd say here, sick of thinking of her body
shredding gently in its wrapper. It's long
enough, I was thinking,
I think too much, it is true, and I wanted to quit myself,
return to the world where the living make
the walls ring. The old woman
held out her hand to me,
she carried her cane in her other hand
and she toed the gravel at the curb
with unease, an edgy foal,
she had the fear old women have of falling —
and then the street began to
widen and evolve
hillocks, jagged canyons, strata,
seasons, constellations that darted and hid their chilled faces
in the skirts of puddles that we
cautiously negotiated, I had forgotten
the organic lushness of the street in slow motion,
the nervous weight of a woman's hand

asking, and I wanted to thank her
before the light changed for filling up the burst hole,
but she said Jesus
always provides, doesn't He? So
I said In a way, ma'am, and You have a good night,
and we parted on the other side, and I left
blessed.

Kaddish

for L.M.K., 1939–1992

Sometimes the traffic as it goes by
is a river, the little steel boxes
bearing our souls home. Sometimes the bedroom window
is the riverbank, and I lie here
hearing many of us scud by, and sometimes, very late,
the fingers of water pluck at the hem of my mother's body
and lead her off, morsel by morsel,
down the open drain of the bath,
the coiled iron pipe of the Niles sewage system,
then the trunk of the river itself. Many bodies join her there,
finally my mama's stopped
feeling lonely, the trolling plankton
nuzzle the shreds of her, my mother
feeds them: it is her bodily nature to be good! And
the two souls of my mother — the child soul in her long agony,
the bitch soul, chewing at the other's arm, the span of its
lifetime suddenly lopped off —
are both dispersed, now, both blended into a film
of particulate dew, ah, my mother kisses the grasses

Blessed be the grasses that bear the weight of those kisses,
Blessed be the arm of the river that pours from the shower head,
Blessed be waters that lave the skin and the souls,
Blessed be the souls of my companions, borne up
upon the river, who sip from the waters and breathe from the dews
and carry with me the taste of her kisses.

About the Author

Sharon Kraus was born in Chicago; she earned her M.A. in Creative Writing from New York University. Her poems have appeared in *Agni, TriQuarterly, Prairie Schooner,* and many other journals. She has been a working scholar at the Bread Loaf Writers' Conference and a recipient of the Editors' Choice award from *Columbia: A Journal of Literature and Art,* an Academy of American Poets prize, and other awards. She is pursuing her Ph.D. in English Literature at the Graduate School of the City University of New York and teaches at Queens College, CUNY.

Recent Titles from Alice James Books

Adrienne Su, *Middle Kingdom*
Ellen Watson, *We Live in Bodies*
Kinereth Gensler, *Journey Fruit*
Cynthia Huntington, *We Have Gone to the Beach*
Nora Mitchell, *Proofreading the Histories*
Ted Deppe, *The Wanderer King*
Robert Cording, *Heavy Grace*
Forrest Hamer, *Call and Response*
E. J. Miller Laino, *Girl Hurt*
Doug Anderson, *The Moon Reflected Fire*
Deborah DeNicola, *Where Divinity Begins*
Richard McCann, *Ghost Letters*
Rita Gabis, *The Wild Field*
Suzanne Matson, *Durable Goods*
David Williams, *Traveling Mercies*
Margaret Lloyd, *This Particular Earthly Scene*
Timothy Liu, *Vox Angelica*
Alice Jones, *The Knot*
Jean Valentine, *The River at Wolf*

Alice James Books has been publishing poetry since 1973. One of the few presses in the country that is run collectively, the cooperative selects manuscripts for publication through competitions. New authors become active members of the press, participating in editorial and production activities. The press, which places an emphasis on publishing women poets, was named for Alice James, sister of William and Henry, whose gift for writing was ignored and whose fine journal did not appear in print until after her death.